ADVANCING THE CONVERSATION ON
RACISM
AND RACIAL
RECONCILIATION

ADVANCING THE CONVERSATION ON
RACISM
AND RACIAL RECONCILIATION

A Liberational-Missional
Theological Primer

DERRICK L. JACKSON

Townsend Press
Nashville, Tennessee

Copyright © 2022 Derrick L. Jackson
All rights reserved.
This book is protected under the copyright laws of the United States of America. No part of this book may be reproduced in any form, stored in a retrieval system, or transmitted in any forum or by any means—electronic, mechanical, photocopying, recording, or any otherwise—without the prior written permission of Dr. Derrick L. Jackson, author and publisher.

Unless otherwise identified, all Scripture quotations are taken from the Holy Bible, NEW INTERNATIONAL VERSION® Copyright © 1973, 1978, 1984, 2011 by Biblica, Inc.® Used by permission. All rights reserved worldwide.

Published by TOWNSEND PRESS
(A division of the Sunday School Publishing Board)
1700 Baptist World Center Drive
Nashville, Tennessee 37207

Printed in the United States of America

ISBN: 978-1-949052-93-0

To all persons who have a heart and passion for
racial justice, racial healing, and racial reconciliation.

CONTENTS

Introduction 9

CHAPTER ONE

    The Greatest Commandment: to Love 11

CHAPTER TWO

    The Weightier Matter of Justice 15

CHAPTER THREE

    The Liberation of the Least of These 19

CHAPTER FOUR

    The Missional Narrative of Scripture 24

        The Trinity 26

        Creation 28

        Jesus' Ministry 30

        Kingdom Vision 32

Conclusion 38

Notes 39

Bibliography 47

Introduction

World-renowned scholar W. E. B. Du Bois declared in his groundbreaking 1903 book *The Souls of Black Folk* that "the problem of the Twentieth Century is the problem of the color-line."[1] Sadly, that profound observation still rings true more than a hundred years later in the twenty-first century. The writer contends that race is not simply one of many problems but a major problem with global implications.[2] Racism is "the prejudgment of and disdain toward others whose racial characteristics are regarded as different, and it is the use of power enforced by legal, cultural, religious, economic, political, and hierarchical structures to isolate and exploit other groups in order to preserve the privileges of a dominant group."[3] It is "not merely an attitude to be converted by religion or a pathology requiring therapy; it is an institutionalized, systemic evil that takes many forms rooted in the assumption that one race is superior to another."[4] In a real sense, racism is "a personal and social disorder" that must be challenged personally and socially.[5]

Bruce Fong is correct when he asserts that "such a recognition of racism calls for deliberate and responsible attention by all people."[6] However, discussions relating to racism and racial reconciliation have often been framed within philosophical, political, psychological, and sociological contexts. The writer, however, contends that the church is God's ideal vehicle to confront racism and advance the conversation of racial healing and reconciliation in the world.

As churches continue to seek to be a missional witness in a pluralistic society and partner with God in His divine mission to redeem, liberate, reconcile, and restore creation, the sin of racism must be addressed. As followers of Jesus Christ, we are called and sent by God to prophetically confront the sin of racism and expand our ministry reach to include efforts to facilitate racial reconciliation that leads to transformation and liberation for individuals and the entire society.

This primer can help churches advance the conversation about racism, racial healing, and racial reconciliation.

The writer, therefore, approaches racial reconciliation through the paradigmatic theme of God's mission to redeem, liberate, reconcile, and restore humanity. What follows is a brief liberational–missional theological framework for discussing racism and the ongoing spiritual process of racial reconciliation in light of the greatest commandment to love, the weightier matter of justice, the liberation of the least of these, and the missional narrative of Scripture.

Take a Minute
Introduction Discussion Questions

1. The writer defines racism in both individual and institutional terms.

    What are some ways you have observed or experienced racism facilitated by the legal system, political system, economic system, and educational system in your community, town, or city?

2. In what ways have you observed or experienced racism facilitated by the church in your community, town, or city?

3. The writer refers to racism not as one of many problems, but as a major problem with global implications. What are some pivotal events today to which your church or ministry has opportunity to respond to racism in all of its nefarious forms?

4. Have you been complicit in facilitating racism? How so?

5. Have you benefited from individual or systemic racism in your life? How so?

CHAPTER ONE

The Greatest Commandment: to Love

The centrality of love to the Christian faith and its value to racial reconciliation was depicted by Jesus when He declared, "'Love the Lord your God with all your heart and with all your soul and with all your mind.' This is the first and greatest commandment. And the second is like it: 'Love your neighbor as yourself.' All the Law and the Prophets hang on these two commandments" (Matthew 22:37-40).[1] The origin of the greatest commandment to love can be traced to Deuteronomy 6:5 and Leviticus 19:18. Both commandments were amalgamated by Jesus to depict the Christian's fundamental standard for living. By combining the two commandments, Jesus illuminated the interrelationship between love for God and love for humanity. One cannot love God without loving humanity, and one cannot love humanity without loving God. Christian love, therefore, is both horizontal and vertical. Emphasizing the centrality of love to the Christian, John declared this:

> We love because he first loved us. Whoever claims to love God yet hates a brother or sister is a liar. For whoever does not love their brother and sister, whom they have seen, cannot love God, whom they have not seen. And he has given us this command: Anyone who loves God must also love their brother and sister (1 John 4:20).

Martin Luther King Jr. reminds us that love is "the supreme unifying principle of life."[2] It is the "*summum bonum* of life which stands at the center of the cosmos."[3] Love is the Christian's active and aggressive response to the ills of society.[4] According to King,

> *Agape* love is not weak, passive love. It is love in action. It is love seeking to preserve and create community. It is insistence on community even when one seeks to break it. *Agape* love is a willingness to go to any length to restore community. It doesn't stop at the first mile, but it goes the second mile to restore community. It is a willingness to forgive, not seven times, but seventy times seven to restore community.[5]

Love is foundational for racial reconciliation. It gives one the spiritual motivation and framework to forgive. In the words of Martin Luther King Jr., "forgiveness means reconciliation, a coming together again."[6] Love, therefore, enables persons and communities to break down individual and institutional racial barriers and repair what was once broken. The converse of love is hate. Hate hinders racial reconciliation. Racism is an expression of hate. It becomes a cancer in the soul of the one who harbors and practices it. Booker T. Washington, in his autobiography *Up from Slavery*, shared the following personal statement concerning hate:

> "It is now long ago that I learned this lesson from General Armstrong, and resolved, that I would permit no man, no matter what his color might be, to narrow and degrade my soul by making me hate him."[7]

Benjamin E. Mays stated, "God has put the black and the white man here in America to prove to the world that two races varying in culture and color can live together, each contributing to the welfare of the other. God, if one lets Him, erases, from one's heart race hatred and prejudice."[8]

According to King, "when we rise to love of agape level, we love men not because we like them, not because their attitudes and ways appeal to us, but because God loves us. Here we rise to the position of loving the person who does the evil deed while hating the deed that the person does."[9] King declared, "Let no man pull you so low as to hate him."[10] King illustrated this conviction when he stated to the racist power structure of Montgomery, Alabama:

> We will match your capacity to inflict suffering with our capacity to endure suffering. We will meet your physical force with soul force. We will not hate you. . . . Do to us what you will and we will still love you. Bomb our homes and threaten our children; send your hooded perpetrators of violence into our communities and drag us out of some wayside road, beating us and leaving us half dead, and we will still love you. But we will soon wear you down with our capacity to suffer. And in winning our freedom we will so appeal to your heart and conscience that will win you in the process.[11]

Love, in a real sense, is active, redemptive, and transformative. It is the force capable of reconciling enemies into friends. It is the power and strength capable of motivating communities to transform unjust institutions into just structures. It is "the highest good and the most durable power in the world."[12] In other words, love is justice in action.

Take a Minute
Chapter One Discussion Questions

1. Do you agree that love is "the Christian's active and aggressive response to the ills of our society" in general and racism in particular? Why or why not? Explain your answer.

2. Do you agree that love equals justice, as alluded to in this chapter? Why or why not? Explain your answer.

3. Dr. Martin Luther King Jr. seemed to espouse a "radical love." Is there a "safe love?" What do you think are the implications of your answer to racism and racial reconciliation?

4. The writer intentionally framed the discussion of racism and racial reconciliation in America within the context of persons of European descent and persons of African descent? Do you agree with this approach? Explain your answer.

Chapter Two
The Weightier Matter of Justice

Pursuing justice is an important characteristic of racial reconciliation. According to King, "Justice is love in calculation; It is love correcting that which revolts against love."[1] Where there is no justice, there is no reconciliation. In the words of Eugene Rivers, "reconciliation divorced from a commitment to truth and justice is a sham."[2] David Gushee adds:

> There can be no racial reconciliation unless there is first the redress of race-based or race-linked injustice, just as there can generally be no reconciliation between alienated persons or groups until or unless previous and current wrongs are constructively addressed.[3]

Succinctly stated, "an inability or unwillingness to recognize systemic racial injustice makes real racial reconciliation all but impossible."[4]

However, one must remember that the God of the Bible is the "God of justice" (Isaiah 30:18). God is not an inactive and abstract deity unconcerned about injustices in the world in general and racial injustice in particular. God is an active and personal God working through humanity to produce justice in the world.[5] King writes:

> Now the fact that this new age is emerging reveals something basic about the universe. It tells us something about the core and the heartbeat of the cosmos. It reminds us that the universe is on the

side of justice. It says to those who struggle for justice, "You do not struggle alone, but God struggles with you." This belief that God is on the side of truth comes down to us from a long tradition of our Christian faith.[6]

The nature and character of God encompass justice. As a result, God calls and demands humanity to prioritize justice. For example, Micah 6:8 declares: "He has shown you, O mortal, what is good. And what does the Lord require of you? To act justly and to love mercy and to walk humbly with your God." Micah echoed the profound theme that living in God's justice is more important than performing the correct sacrificial rituals before God (Micah 6:6-7).

The verb used for "require" is the Hebrew word *doresh,* an active participle. This verb form demonstrates action being done in an uninterrupted state—it neither starts nor stops. It is never-ending, showing that the action defined by the verb is to be going on all the time. Hence, pursuing justice is to be the ongoing pursuit of the Christian. In commenting on justice, Walter Brueggemann states:

> Justice is to sort out what belongs to whom, and to return it to them. Such an understanding implies that there is a right distribution of goods and access to the sources of life. There are certain entitlements which cannot be mocked. Yet through the uneven workings of the historical process, some come to have access to or control of what belongs to others. If we control what belongs to others long enough, we come to think of it as rightly ours, and to forget it belonged to someone else. So the work of liberation, redemption, salvation, is the work of giving things back.[7]

In speaking of justice for blacks in America, King writes:

> Absolute justice for the Negro simply means, in the Aristotelian sense, that the Negro must have his

due. A society that has done something against the Negro for hundreds of years must now do something special for him in order to equip him to compete on a just and equal basis."[8]

The theme of justice is also seen in Leviticus 25:10, which asserts: "Consecrate the fiftieth year and proclaim liberty throughout the land to all its inhabitants. It shall be a jubilee for you; each of you is to return to your family property and to your own clan." In commenting on this verse, Maria Harris suggests: "the particular meaning of justice that Jubilee stresses is the notion of 'return,' not in the Jubilee journey sense of a return home but return as relinquishing, giving back, and handing over what is not ours to God and to those crying for justice throughout the whole, round earth."[9]

Additionally, the importance of justice is seen in the Zacchaeus story where Luke writes:

> But Zacchaeus stood up and said to the Lord, "Look, Lord! Here and now I give half of my possessions to the poor, and if I have cheated anybody out of anything, I will pay back four times the amount." Jesus said to him, "Today salvation has come to this house, because this man, too, is a son of Abraham. For the Son of Man came to seek and to save the lost." (Luke 19:8-10)

While the concepts of repentance and salvation are often highlighted when commenting on this story, it is important to remember that Zacchaeus was applauded by Jesus for wanting to make right the wrongs that others experienced at his hands. In other words, Zacchaeus was commended by Jesus for wanting to do justice.

Jesus also placed a premium on pursuing justice when he declared in Matthew 23:23: "Woe to you, teachers of the law and Pharisees, you hypocrites! You give a tenth of your spices—mint, dill and cumin. But you have neglected the more important matters of the law—justice, mercy and faithfulness. You should have practiced the latter, without neglecting the former." Jesus teaches that religious rituals unaccompanied by deep concerns and actions for justice are not received by him. Additionally, the observation of the smallest details of the law while neglecting the weightier matter of justice will not be accepted by him. In a real sense, Jesus declares that religious worship, church polity, personal piety, soul care, and other spiritual activities cannot be substituted for pursuing the weightier matter of justice. Pursuing justice, and therefore pursuing racial reconciliation, is one of the weightier matters of Scripture.

Take a Minute
Chapter Two Discussion Questions

1. The writer suggests that where there is no justice, there is no reconciliation. David Gushee maintains that racial reconciliation void of redress of race-based injustice is not reconciliation at all. Have you observed efforts to reconcile that are divorced from the hard work of justice and redress? Please explain.

2. The writer suggests that pursuing justice, and thereby pursuing racial reconciliation, is one of the weightier matters of Scripture? Do you agree? Why or why not? How do you reconcile (if you can) the writer's position with the Great Commission?

3. Does your church or ministry highlight certain moral or cultural sins as more significant than other sins in general and the sin of racism in particular? If so, give examples and discuss why you feel that is the case.

4. Has your church or ministry played a role in challenging racism or permeating and prolonging racism? Please explain.

5. Do you, your church, or your ministry practice "sophisticated racism?"

6. How does that phrase make you feel? Please explain.

Chapter Three
The Liberation of the Least of These

Racial reconciliation is not only an individual endeavor; it is also a societal responsibility. Limiting racial reconciliation to individual expressions limits racial equality throughout society. Racial reconciliation, therefore, encompasses liberation, and liberation involves the sharing of power and resources. In the United States, "only one racial group has the power to impose its will upon and exploit other racial groups, and only one racial group has the power to pretend that racism does not exist."[1] Whites, as a racial group, control power and resources in America. When whites share power and resources with blacks, it is an acknowledgment of the lingering effects of racism and a display of societal repentance.

Interestingly, John the Baptist reminds us in a discussion on repentance of the importance of "doing specific, concrete political and economic acts as signs of our turning toward God (Luke 3:7-18)."[2] Shared power and resources between blacks and whites assist in developing a shared future based upon the kingdom of God. In discussing the lack of power of blacks in the black and white relationship, King asserts:

> One of the great problems that the Negro confronts is his lack of power. From the old plantations of the South to the newer ghettos of the North, the Negro has been confined to a life of voicelessness and powerlessness.... The plantation and ghetto were created by those who had power, both to confine those who had no power and to perpetuate their powerlessness. The problem of transforming the ghetto, therefore, is a problem of power.[3]

In a real sense, power is an extension of love and justice. Power, love, and justice are interrelated. In commenting on the interconnectedness of love, justice, and power, King writes:

> Power, properly understood, is the ability to achieve purpose. It is the strength required to bring about social, political or economic changes. In this sense power is not only desirable but necessary in order to implement the demands of love and justice. . . . What is needed is a realization that power without love is reckless and abusive and love without power is sentimental and anemic. Power at its best is love implementing the demands of justice. Justice at its best is love correcting everything that stands against love.[4]

Power, therefore, understood through a kingdom agenda liberates both the steward of power and the community where power is exercised. Hence, shared power and resources between blacks and whites within a kingdom framework facilitates racial reconciliation in a fashion whereby relationships are affirmed based on dignity and equality and resources are allocated based on fairness and equity. King, however, cautions: "Power is not the white man's birthright; it will not be legislated for us and delivered in neat government packages. It is a social force any group can utilize by accumulating its elements in a planned, deliberate campaign to organize it under its own control."[5]

The sharing of power liberates racial victims of social, economic, educational, and political oppression and exploitation.[6] Jesus declared in Matthew 25:40, "Truly I tell you, whatever you did for one of the least of these brothers and sisters of mine, you did for me." The mandate of Jesus includes black brothers and sisters whom society relegates as least among it by racist structures, practices, and attitudes. Unfortunately, many turn a blind eye to the racial inequalities of the "least of these," while others blame the victim of systemic racism for racial injustice. Nicholas Wolterstorff writes:

> There are many explanations of failing to see the faces and hear the voices of those who are wronged, even of those right before one. Sometimes we loathe the victims. Sometimes we are overwhelmed by the fear of what we would have to do if we genuinely saw and heard; so we block out the sight and muffle the sound. And sometimes our frameworks of conviction lead us to discount the significance of what we see and hear. We regard the one before us as a candidate for charity, should we be so inclined; or we insist that his condition is his own fault. We resist acknowledging that the presence of the other before us places a claim on us, issues to us a call to do justice.[7]

Kenneth Greene adds:

> Whites assume the victims themselves cause their problems rather than the institutions of the victimizers. And Whites assume that the cure for black illnesses begins with them and needs to be administered by whites. And then, to add the final blow, the very institutions that created the problem in the first place administrate the "cure."[8]

In speaking of the strategy of oppressors, Wolterstorff states, "Oppressors do all they can to prevent the use of the category of justice; they do all they can to cast the situation in terms of 'better and worse' rather than 'justice and injustice.'"[9] In other words, many benefactors of unjust racial structures struggle to discuss racism from an institutional perspective. Some dislike and dismiss the conversation altogether. For many of them, the remedy for oppression in general and racism, in particular, is solely an individual effort. Jesus, however, emphasized liberation at both the individual and institutional levels (Luke 4:18-19). Reconciliation, therefore, includes liberation. As James Cone writes:

> Fellowship with God is made possible through God's activity in history, setting people free from economic, social, and political bondage. God's act of reconciliation is not mystical communion with the divine; nor is it a pietistic state of inwardness bestowed upon the believer. God's reconciliation is a new relationship with *people* created by God's concrete involvement in the political affairs of the world, taking sides with the weak and the helpless.[10]

In discussing the connection between liberation and reconciliation, J. Deotis Roberts states:

> Reconciliation is always to be placed in conjunction with liberation. What we seek is a liberating experience of reconciliation. . . . It is an urgent responsibility thrust upon us that we seek to "heal our land" by purging it of racism.[11]

In other words, the same God who saves and reconciles is the same God who liberates. Jesus, therefore, is our savior, liberator, and reconciler.[12]

Take a Minute
Chapter Three Discussion Questions

1. The writer suggests that there is a connection between liberation and reconciliation. According to the writer, you cannot have one without the other. Do you agree? Why or why not?

2. Do you feel that white privilege is a barrier to liberation and, therefore a barrier to racial reconciliation? Does white privilege blind some persons to racism and the need for racial reconciliation? Please expound on your answer.

3. What are your thoughts concerning the "dirty word" *reparations*? Are reparations necessary for reconciliation? If so, what would reparations look like in the twenty-first century?

4. How do you respond to others who maintain that America suffers from "racism talk fatigue" and that the country would be better served if we did not talk about race so much?

CHAPTER FOUR
The Missional Narrative of Scripture

There is a grand narrative to Scripture that helps one discern how racism is antithetical to the Christian story. The overarching story of Scripture embraces "the whole of creation, time, and humanity within its scope, and it invites one to live into the mission of God."[1] God's mission is the central focus of Scripture,[2] and God's mission is to redeem, liberate, reconcile, and restore creation. Writers such as N. T. Wright and Christopher Wright suggest that the mission of God unfolds in a "five-act drama" that includes the Creation, the Fall, Israel, Christ, and the New Creation.[3] Other writers such as Craig Bartholomew and Michael W. Goheen posit that the mission of God unfolds in a "six-act drama that includes the Creation, the Fall, redemption initiated, redemption accomplished, the mission of the church, and redemption completed."[4]

Regardless of the categories, the grand narrative of Scripture portrays a God who is actively working toward "making all things new" (Revelation 21:1). Michael Gorman writes, "The scriptures of both testaments bear witness to a God who, as creator and redeemer of the world, is already on mission seeking not to just save souls to take to heaven someday, but to restore and save the created order."[5] Hence, while sin is the tension in the overall narrative, it is not the nucleus of the story. The creating, redeeming, liberating, reconciling, and restoring acts of God are the main storylines of Scripture.

In the grand narrative of Scripture, the triune God calls and sends Abraham, Israel, Jesus Christ, and the church to facilitate God's redeeming, liberating, reconciling, and restoring purposes in the world where all creation flourishes in the peaceable kingdom of God.[6] John provides a vision of creation flourishing in the kingdom of God:

> Then I saw a new heaven and a new earth; for the first heaven and the first earth had passed away, and the sea was no more. And I saw the holy city, the new Jerusalem, coming down out of heaven from God, prepared as a bride adorned for her husband. And I heard a loud voice from the throne saying, "See, the home of God is among mortals. He will dwell with them; they will be his peoples, and God himself will be with them." (Revelation 21:1-3)

The writer maintains that humanity is currently experiencing the part of God's drama where the church has been called and sent by God to participate in the divine mission to liberate and reconcile creation to its intended purpose.[7] The church, therefore, should take the lead in opposing racism in all its forms and advancing the conversation of race and racial reconciliation.[8] As sociologist George Yancey argues:

> Christians must begin to take the leadership role because our faith offers a unique answer to racism. If we can take the moral lead, we will provide a powerful witness to all those who are frustrated by racial problems in the United States. There could be few greater miracles in our society than to find a solution to racial alienation. I contend that there is a unique Christian perspective different from the solutions offered by the non-Christian world. We need dialogue among many Christians to begin to develop a faith-based voice.[9]

God's mission to and for the world as revealed through a Trinitarian understanding of God provides an initial foundation for denouncing racism and promoting racial reconciliation.

The Trinity

God's mission is grounded in the relational and substantive nature of the Trinity.[10] Some approach the Trinity with an Augustine emphasis on how God could be one and three at the same time. Others approach the Trinity with a Moltmann view of the way the three persons of the Godhead function and relate to each other as one.[11] Relying on John of Damascus' concept of "Perichoresis," Moltmann argues that the Trinity is best understood as the Godhead of Father, Son, and Spirit, who mutually and equally indwell each other for missional service.[12] Moltmann formulated a doctrine of the Trinity that "rested on his bold claim that Trinitarian fellowship not only describes divine community but also prescribes the nature of true human community."[13] The Trinity, therefore, offers an invitation "to share in this dynamic communion of love by offering to them its very essence—the creative capacity to love others."[14] The writer maintains that Moltmann's approach to the Trinity is the better one because it depicts a God who is "a community of Father, Son, and Spirit, and whose unity is constituted by mutual indwelling and reciprocal interpenetration rather than a God who is an abstract monotheist."[15] This view of the Trinity emphasizes a God who values communion and equality. Veli-Matti Karkakainen writes, "If there is one crucial development concerning the Trinity on which all Christian theologians are currently in agreement, it is the rise to prominence of the understanding of God as communion."[16] Amos Yong suggests this:

> At the center of the universe is a relationship, a community of love, a plurality within a unified being. As the famous symbol presents, the Father is not the Son and the Son is not the Spirit and the Spirit is not the Father. However, the Father, Son, and Spirit comprise the one being of God.[17]

The Trinity, therefore, consists of "three divine and equal persons of the Godhead: Father, Son, and Spirit who do not exist outside of each other, but rather, they find their existence in each other in revealing God's concept of community." Moltmann further writes:

> By virtue of their perichoresis, the divine persons exist so intimately with one another, for one another, and in one another that they constitute a single . . . unity by themselves. This is the Trinitarian concept of the unity of the triune God, because it combines threeness and oneness without reducing the three to one or the one to three.[18]

The writer is aware that the Bible does not utilize the word *Trinity* in portraying the Godhead. However, the Bible does provide portraits of the "perichoretic relationship" of the Godhead. For example, Jesus is portrayed as *in* communion with God *through* the power of the Holy Spirit in Luke 3:22. Jesus said to his disciples, "Believe me that I am *in* the Father and the Father is *in* me" (John 14:11). In speaking of the Holy Spirit's involvement in the triune relationship, Jesus said, "But the Helper, the Holy Spirit, whom the Father will send *in* my name, He will teach you all things" (John 14:26). In the creation story, God said, "Let *us* make mankind in *our* image, in *our* likeness" (Gen. 1:26). Hence, the divine relationality of the Trinity invites us to live equally and relationally with one another without surrendering our own distinctiveness as we live in the divine *perichoresis* of God. In reflecting upon this concept, Dwight Zschiele reminds us:

> The life of genuine mutuality of the three persons of the Trinity invites us to affirm the full humanity and giftedness of others around us as God-given and vital not only for the world's well-being and growth, but for ours too. In a Trinitarian perspective, otherness is not to be erased, diminished or overwhelmed, but rather treasured and enhanced within the pattern of a larger unity and purpose. Thus, reconciled diversity, not uniformity or division, becomes normative for a Trinitarian understanding of human community.[19]

The Trinity, therefore, reflects God's desire for a communal relationship based upon love, equality, dignity, sacredness, and mutuality. Reconciliation is rooted in the "distinctively Christian understanding of God as Triune—Father, Son, and Holy Spirit."[20] Racial reconciliation, therefore, flows from the Trinitarian nature and activity of God. Racism, on the other hand, disrupts "the interrelatedness of life, the sacredness of human personality, the moral order of the universe."[21] It reflects a distortion of communal relationship and a destruction of equality and dignity initiated by God in creation.

Creation

God's desire for relationship resulted in God creating the world. Genesis portrays a God who created the cosmos for relationship.[22] The first three Hebraic words of Genesis are *B'reishit bara Elohim* (In the Beginning, Created, God). God's nature and mission is to be in relationship with His creation. The creation narrative in Genesis depicts a God who created humanity for harmonious community. Racism disrupts the communal relationship God desired for humanity. It works against the harmonious community God preferred for all human beings. According to Martin Luther King Jr., "he who works against community works against creation."[23] In a real sense, racism disrupts the "relational wholeness" of creation, and it denies creation's principle of "divine and human interrelatedness."[24]

The creation narrative also depicts a God who placed premium value on all humanity. Genesis states: "So God created mankind in his own image, in the image of God he created them; male and female he created them" (Genesis 1:27). Humanity is the crowning jewel of God's creation. Human beings are created in the image of God *(imago Dei)*.[25] As a result, humans become image-bearers of God in the world.[26] Racism denies the fact that all human beings are created in the image of God with inherent dignity and worth. It distorts humanity's capacity to fully image God through the lens of "the other." In actuality, racism diminishes the full humanity of others, and devalues the giftedness of all human beings. Martin Luther King Jr. reminds us:

> Our Hebraic-Christian tradition refers to the inherent dignity of man in the Biblical phrase the *image of God*. This innate worth referred to in the phrase the image of God is universally shared in equal proportions by all men. There is no graded scale of essential worth; there is no divine right of one race which differs from the divine right of another. Every human being has etched in his personality the indelible stamp of the Creator.[27]

For King, the sin of racism is diametrically opposed to God's stamp of sacredness on all of humanity. Utilizing the racist system of segregation to illustrate his point, King writes:

> Segregation stands diametrically opposed to the principle of the sacredness of human personality. It debases personality. . . . So long as the Negro is a means to an end, so long as he is seen as anything less than a person of sacred worth, the image of God is abused in him and consequently and proportionally lost by those who inflict and abuse.[28]

Racism represents a corrupt view of creation. It contradicts the creation narrative that suggests that all persons have a common genesis with inherent dignity and worth bestowed upon them by God. It contradicts God's divine act of creating all persons in His image to become equal and harmonious image-bearers of God. Racism also destroys the harmonious relationship God desired, and it creates tremendous human pain. In highlighting the negative effects of racism, Vanderbilt University Divinity School states:

> Racism hurts human beings. It erodes the soul of those who oppress; it humiliates its victims. Racism creates in oppressors a false sense of superiority; in victims it creates an equally false sense of inferiority. Racism enlarges the rage of those it denies; it is profoundly painful for those it demeans. A huge hurt lives in the heart of those who are racially oppressed.[29]

In essence, racism is inconsistent with God's design for creation. God desired harmonious relationship between all creation. The Garden of Eden was "God's original sanctuary of dwelling for harmonious relationship with all of creation."[30] However, sin disrupted this exemplary relationship resulting in the fall of all humanity. As a result, the Savior was sent to redeem humanity and began the process of liberation, reconciliation and restoration.

Jesus' Ministry

God came to humanity in the person of Jesus Christ to redeem, liberate and reconcile humanity. The death, burial, and resurrection of Jesus Christ gave humanity the opportunity to be redeemed, liberated and reconciled to God and to each other. Jesus manifested God in the flesh and continued the redemptive, liberating, reconciling, and restoring mission of God. John said, "The Word became flesh and made his dwelling among us" (John 1:14).

Some contend that Jesus' only purpose for coming into the world was to die for the sins of humanity. The writer, however, contends that Jesus Christ not only came into the world incarnate to die for the sins of the world, but He also came into the world to advance the kingdom of God, which will result in a reordering of relationships and a realigning of systems under the reign and rule of God.[31] According to Donald Kraybill, "The genius of the incarnation is that spiritual and social worlds intersect in Jesus Christ. To separate them is to deny the incarnation. Social and spiritual are inextricably woven together in the Jesus story."[32] N. T. Wright maintains that "Jesus came into the world to launch God's new creation . . . to rehumanize human beings . . . where they rediscover what they have been made for, what Israel had been created for."[33]

In teaching His disciples, Jesus declared in the Model Prayer recorded, "Your kingdom come and your will be done on earth as it is in heaven" (Matthew 6:9-13). With that statement, Jesus made the spiritual and the social two sides of the same coin. Jesus' ministry challenged both the personal sin of racism and the institutional sin of racism. For example, Jesus' interaction with the Samaritan woman in John 4:1-15 illustrated his opposition to racism and his desire to break down racial barriers. In associating with the Samaritan woman, Jesus challenged the Jewish belief of superiority, and He exposed the Jewish practice of segregation. By connecting with the Samaritan woman, Jesus affirmed her humanity, and he disclosed her dignity. In essence, Jesus' actions rebutted the personal and institutional racist attitudes and actions of the Jews.

In Matthew 28:18-20, Jesus instructed his disciples to share the Gospel with all humanity, thereby suggesting that all human beings have equal access to the Gospel. Jesus' public ministry, as illustrated in the Sermon on the Mount narrative, reflected an emphasis on equality, justice, peace, community and love. Racism contradicts Jesus's admonition to love. Jesus declared: "You shall love the Lord your God with all your heart, all your soul, and with all your strength, and with all your mind; and your neighbor as yourself" (Luke 10:27). Racism is inconsistent with Christ's goal of reconciliation. Paul writes:

> But now in Christ Jesus you who once were far away have been brought near by the blood of Christ. For he himself is our peace, who has made the two groups one and has destroyed the barrier, the dividing wall of hostility, by setting aside in his flesh the law with its commands and regulations. His purpose was to create in himself one new humanity out of the two, thus making peace, and in one body to reconcile both of them to God through the cross, by which he put to death their hostility. (Ephesians 2:13-16)

The cross of Jesus Christ illustrated God's desire to liberate humanity from "all forms of oppression and domination,"[34] particularly the oppression of racism and the domination of racist systems. The cross of Jesus, however, "was not good news for the powerful, for those who are comfortable with the way things are, or for anyone whose understanding of religion is aligned with power."[35] Nevertheless,

Jesus' earthly ministry ended on the cross to illustrate the premium God placed on redemption, liberation and reconciliation. The cross, therefore, was a powerful symbol of the possibility of reconciliation in general and racial reconciliation between blacks and whites in particular. James Cone writes:

> No two people in America have had more violent and loving encounters than black and white people. We were made brothers and sisters by the blood of the lynching tree . . . and the blood of the cross of Jesus. No gulf between blacks and whites is too great to overcome, for our beauty is more enduring than our brutality. What God joined together, no one can tear apart.[36]

Failure to oppose racism and pursue racial reconciliation is failure to "walk in the way of the Lord."[37] Such failure is contrary to the vision of the kingdom.

Kingdom Vision

The kingdom of God was heralded by the birth, life, death, and resurrection of Jesus Christ. Unlike some who believe that the kingdom of God is exclusively future tense, with no relevance for presence, or totally present tense with no hope for the future, the writer maintains that the kingdom of God is both present and future.[38] God's kingdom is "neither the future of time nor timeless eternity. It is the future-made-present creating new conditions for possibilities in history."[39] The kingdom vision speaks both of a "coming God" and a God "who has already arrived."[40] Hence, followers of Jesus Christ live in the tension of the "now" and the "not yet," with the understanding that Christ inaugurated the kingdom at His first coming and will consummate the kingdom during his second coming.

The kingdom of God is the "dynamic rule and reign of God made up of persons who have yielded their hearts and relationships to the reign of God".[41] It is characterized by an "upside-down" reality in which "the Kingdom establishes a new order of things that looks upside-down in the diverse cultures around the world today just as it looked upside-down in the midst of the Palestinian culture in the first century."[42] To illustrate Jesus' upside-down kingdom approach, Donald B. Kraybill writes:

> Jesus was faced with the right-side-up option of establishing a political kingship using violent force or coercive power. However, Jesus utilized the upside-down approach of using humble service as the new way of ruling: "his upside-down revolution replaced force with suffering and violence with love. Jesus faced the right-side-up option of endorsing institutionalized religion and receiving its accolades. Jesus responded, however, with the upside-down critique of established religion stale practices. When Jesus was faced with the right-side options of either responding violently or miraculously to end economic oppression, Jesus responded upside-down by redefining what it meant to be truly rich and calling those with abundance to stop hoarding and give generously.[43]

The kingdom vision, therefore, includes making all things new as depicted in Christ's resurrection and illustrated by baptism. In God's kingdom, "there is no longer Jew or Greek, there is no longer slave or free, there is no longer male and female; for all are one in Christ Jesus" (Galatians 3:28). The "dividing wall of hostility" (Ephesians 2:14) is brought down in the kingdom. As God rules and reigns, "the last will be first, and the first will be last" (Matthew 20:16). God's kingdom vision is an alternative vision that challenges the abuse of power of the status quo,[44] and it exposes efforts of division by the culture.[45] The kingdom of God was the main thrust of Jesus' life.[46] Jesus stated, "The Spirit of the Lord is on me, because he has anointed me to preach good news to the poor. He has sent me to proclaim freedom for the prisoners and recovery of sight for the blind, to release the oppressed, to proclaim the year of the Lord's favor" (Luke 4:18-19). The kingdom vision, therefore, is a liberating vision that promotes personal and societal liberation from racism. It exposes the "moral evil of racial oppression," and it depicts a God who is active in liberating humanity from all forms of oppression.[47] According to Forrest Harris, the kingdom vision encompasses "the reign of God where the world is free of racism, injustice, and oppression, and there is an active relationship between people and God wherein social and political structures are humanized toward total liberation."[48] The writer maintains that freedom from racism is a key aspect of liberation and a major theme of God's alternative vision for the world. While liberation is a key aspect of the kingdom, the writer maintains that reconciliation is at the heart of liberation in the kingdom vision. Racism hinders liberation and reconciliation. It does not reflect the kingdom's liberating vision. It facilitates oppression instead of promoting freedom. Racism undergirds society's wall of hostility instead of destroying the barriers of racial hostility. It maintains the current order of racial domination instead of ushering in the new order of community. Racism "excludes." The kingdom vision "includes." In short, racism is a personal and societal sin incompatible with the kingdom vision. It denies the consummation of human history:

> And they sang a new song: You are worthy to take the scroll and to open its seals, because you were slain, and with your blood you purchased men for God from every tribe and language and people and nation. You have made them to be a kingdom and priests to serve our God, and they will reign on the earth. (Revelation 5:9-10)

In God's alternative vision for the world, the church plays a vital role in confronting racism and promoting racial reconciliation. Despite the fact that "the church is more known for its racial separation and conformity to society's patterns rather than representing a new way of life, a new order of community, or a new value of equality,"[49] the church was founded upon the basic principle that "all dividing walls have been destroyed by Christ's death."[50] Highlighting the church's call to continue the reconciling mission of Christ, Paul states:

> Therefore, if anyone is in Christ, the new creation has come: The old has gone, the new is here! All this is from God, who reconciled us to himself through Christ and gave us the ministry of reconciliation: that God was reconciling the world to himself in Christ, not counting people's sins against them. And he has committed to us the message of reconciliation. We are therefore Christ's ambassadors, as though God were making his appeal through us. We implore you on Christ's behalf: Be reconciled to God. (2 Corinthians 5:17-20)

The church is God's vehicle for making a kingdom impact upon the world. Lesslie Newbigin reminds us that "the primary reality of which we have to take account in seeking for a Christian impact on public life is the Christian congregation."[51] The mission of the church is shaped by the birth, life, death, and resurrection of Jesus. The kingdom vision depicts the church as God's witnesses who live out "God's mission of relationship, redemption, and reconciliation in the world."[52]

The church, therefore, is called to "live in the now and reflect the not yet" at the same time.[53] In the kingdom vision, the church is "the community of God's people who live into the imagination that they are, by their very nature, God's missionary people living as a demonstration of what God plans to do in and for all of creation in Jesus Christ."[54] Therefore, opposing racism and participating in the ongoing spiritual journey of racial reconciliation is central to the mission of the church as it reflects God's kingdom vision. Racism denies equality, inclusion, and love. Racial reconciliation, however, promotes the right ordering of relationships and structures based upon love, equality, and inclusion. The writer maintains that James Cone was correct when he stated that "a right ordering of relationships will result when the church, both black and white church, speak to justice issues such as poverty, quality of life disparities, health disparities, educational disparities, economic disparities, and other justice issues."[55]

The church is called and sent by God to speak out prophetically against all "isms" in our society, notwithstanding the sin of racism. Racism is a personal and systemic evil. It opposes God's commandment to love. It distorts God's call for justice, and it minimizes God's vision of liberation. Racism contradicts God's mission of redemption, reconciliation, and restoration, evidenced in the missional narrative of Scripture. It destroys God's desire for harmonious and equal relationships among all races as reflected in the Trinity, and it distorts the *imago dei* reality as revealed in the creation narrative. Additionally, racism perverts the message and meaning of the cross, and undermines the peaceful, just, liberating, and transforming motif of the kingdom of God. The church, therefore, has a vital role to play in confronting racism and promoting racial reconciliation in our culture. During a public conversation on racial reconciliation, Dr. Jerry Young, president of the National Baptist Convention, USA Inc., stated: "I am convinced that if we don't get this racism issue right in the church, I don't think there's any way we can do it in the culture."[56] Racial reconciliation is a Gospel issue. Therefore, it is a church mandate.

Take a Minute
Chapter Four Discussion Questions

1. The writer maintains that God's mission is the central focus of Scripture, and that mission is to redeem, liberate, reconcile, and restore creation. Do you agree with the writer's assertion? Why or why not?

2. How can the framework mentioned above be useful in the march toward racial reconciliation? Please explain.

3. Describe in your own words how a Trinitarian understanding of God provides an initial foundation for denouncing racism and promoting racial reconciliation.

4. Describe in your own words how the creation narrative is paramount to the discussion of racism and racial reconciliation?

5. How is racism antithetical to the ministry of Jesus? Please explain.

6. How is racism in all of its nefarious forms incompatible with the kingdom vision espoused in Scripture? Please explain.

7. After reading this primer? What are your next steps?

    Do you think there is value in you, your church, or your ministry having a conversation partner on the journey toward racial healing and racial reconciliation? Why or why not?

Conclusion

This primer endeavored to provide a brief liberational-missional theological framework for confronting individual and systemic racism. While this primer is not an exhaustive treatment of the subject matter, the writer endeavored to provide a framework for advancing the conversation of racial injustice, racial healing and racial reconciliation.

The writer believes that the church in general, has a unique opportunity to seize the moment and lead the conversation of racial injustice, racial healing, and racial reconciliation. While racial reconciliation is an ongoing process, the writer believes that it is a heavenly summons that Christians cannot ignore.

Although it is a challenging and difficult task, the writer believes that racial reconciliation is a divine calling with cosmic ramifications, and he is motivated to participate with God in this earthly and eternal journey. The writer invites others who share the same conviction to do likewise.

By nature, the writer is a pragmatist. He sees himself as an "optimistic realist" who still believes in the church and who still has faith in America's potential to become a more racially just society. It is his prayer and hope that this primer will be utilized to inform, inspire, and invite others to participate in God's redeeming and ongoing work of racial reconciliation.

Notes

INTRODUCTION

1. W. E. B. Du Bois, *The Souls of Black Folk* (Chicago, IL: A. C. McClurg & Co., 1903), 19.

2. Bruce W. Fong, "Addressing the Issue of Racial Reconciliation according to the Principles of Ephesians 2:11-22," *JETS 38*, no. 4 (December 1995): 565-80.

3. Vanderbilt University Divinity School, "Toward the Elimination of Racism in Vanderbilt Divinity School and the Graduate Department of Religion," divinity.vanderbilt.edu. http://divinity.vanderbilt.edu/student-life/BlackSeminarians-ELIMINATIONOFRACISM-2006.pdf (accessed January 15, 2017).

4. Ibid.

5. Ibid.

6. Fong, "Addressing the Issue of Racial Reconciliation," 565.

CHAPTER ONE
THE GREATEST COMMANDMENT: TO LOVE

1. The "Greatest Commandment" is depicted in Matthew 22:37-40; Mark 12:29-31; and Luke 10:25-28. John corroborates the prominence of the commandment by referring to it as the "New Commandment" in John 13:34-35.

2. Martin Luther King Jr., *Strength to Love* (New York: Harper & Row, 1963), 38, 43. (Note: The writer relies heavily on Martin Luther King Jr.'s writings in this subsection.)

3. King, *A Testament of Hope: The Essential Writings and Speeches of Martin Luther King, Jr.,* ed. James M. Washington (New York: Harper Collins, 1986), 11.

4. King, *Strength,* 38-43.

5. King, *A Testament of Hope,* 20.

6. King, *Strength,* 50-51.

7. Booker T. Washington, *Up from Slavery* (New York: Oxford University Press, 1901), 97.

8. Benjamin E. Mays, *The Negro's God As Reflected in His Literature* (New York, NY: Atheneum, 1969), 149.

9. King, *Strength,* 52.

10. King, "The Most Durable Power," *A Testament of Hope,* 20.

11. Martin Luther King Jr., *Stride toward Freedom: The Montgomery Story* (New York: Harper Collins Press, reprint 1987), 217.

12. King, *A Testament of Hope,* 20.

CHAPTER TWO
THE WEIGHTIER MATTER OF JUSTICE

1. Martin Luther King Jr., "MIA Mass Meeting at Holt Street Baptist Church," *The Papers of Martin Luther King Jr.,* edited by Clayborne Carson, vol. 3, *Birth of a New Age* December 1955–December 1956 (Berkeley: University of California Press, 1992), 71.

2. Eugene Rivers, "The Responsibility of Evangelical Intellectuals in the Age of White Supremacy," in *The Gospel in Black and White: Theological Resources for Racial Reconciliation,* edited by Dennis L. Okholm (Downers Grove, IL: InterVarsity Press, 1997), 14.

3. David P. Gushee, "Racism and Justice," *Moral Leadership: News and Notes from the Center for Christian Leadership* 2, 4 (2001), http://www.uu.edu/centers/christld/moralld/article.cfm?ArticleID=34 (accessed March 1, 2017).

4. Ibid.

5. King, "Our God Is Able," in *Strength to Love*, 124-32.

6. Martin Luther King Jr., "Facing the Challenge of a New Age," *Phylon* 18 (April 1957): 31.

7. Walter Brueggemann, "Voices of the Night—Against Justice," *To Act Justly, Love Tenderly, Walk Humbly*, Walter Brueggemann, Sharon Park, and Thomas H. Groom (New York: Paulist Press, 1986), 5.

8. Martin Luther King Jr., *Where Do We Go from Here: Chaos or Community?* (New York: Bantam. 1968), 90.

9. Maria Harris, *Proclaim Jubilee! A Spirituality for the Twenty-first Century* (Louisville, KY: Westminster John Knox Press, 1996), 79.

CHAPTER THREE
THE LIBERATION OF THE LEAST OF THESE

1. National Education Association, *Education and Racism* (Washington, 1973) as referenced in Kenneth R. Greene, "Justice and Racism: What White Churches and Institutions Need to Hear," in *Unfinished Reconciliation: Justice, Racism, and Churches of Christ*, Gary Holloway and John York, eds. (Abilene, TX: Abilene Christian University Press, 2013), 165.

2. Kenneth R. Greene, "Justice and Racism: What White Churches and Institutions Need to Hear," in *Unfinished Reconciliation: Justice, Racism, and Churches of Christ*, Gary Holloway and John York, eds. (Abilene, TX: Abilene Christian University Press, 2013), 164.

3. Martin Luther King, Jr., "Where Do We Go from Here," in *A Testament of Hope: The Essential Writings and Speeches of Martin Luther King, Jr.*, ed. James M. Washington (New York: Harper Collins, 1986), 246.

4. King, *Where Do We Go from Here*, 37.

5. Martin Luther King Jr., "Black Power Defined," *I Have a Dream:*

Writings and Speeches That Changed the World, ed. James M. Washington (New York: Harper San Francisco, 1992), 165.

6. James Cone, *A Black Theology of Liberation* (Maryknoll, NY: Orbis, 1986), 2.

7. Nicholas Wolterstorff, *Justice: Rights and Wrongs* (Princeton, NJ: Princeton University Press, 2008), ix.

8. Greene, "Justice and Racism," in *Unfinished Reconciliation*, 167.

9. Wolterstorff, *Justice: Rights and Wrongs*, viii.

10. James Cone, *God of the Oppressed*, rev. ed. (Maryknoll, NY: Orbis, 1997), 209.

11. J. Deotis Roberts, *A Black Political Theology* (Philadelphia, PA: Westminster Press, 1974), 220.

12. Ibid., 221-22.

CHAPTER FOUR
THE MISSIONAL NARRATIVE OF SCRIPTURE

1. Christopher J. H. Wright, *The Mission of God: Unlocking the Bible's Grand Narrative* (Downers Grove, IL: IVP Academic, 2006), 55.

2. Alan J. Roxburgh, *Missional: Joining God in the Neighborhood* (Grand Rapids, MI: Eerdmans, 1998), 11-12.

3. N. T. Wright, *The New Testament and the People of God* (London: SPCK Publishing, 1992).

4. Craig G. Bartholomew and Michael W. Goheen, *The True Story of the Whole World: Finding Your Place in the Biblical Drama* (Grand Rapids, MI: Faith Alive Christian Resources, 2009), 35.

5. Michael Gorman, *Elements of Biblical Exegesis: A Basic Guide for Students and Ministers,* revised and expanded edition (Grand Rapids, MI: Baker, 2009), 155.

6. Michael W. Goheen, *A Light to the Nations: The Missional*

Church and the Biblical Story (Grand Rapids, MI: Baker Academic, 2011), 190-97.

7. Ibid.

8. Ibid., 197.

9. George Yancey, *Beyond Racial Gridlock: Embracing Mutual Responsibility* (Downers Grove, IL: IVP Books, 2006), 12-13.

10. Leonard E. Hjalmarson, "A Trinitarian Spirituality of Mission," *Journal of Spiritual Formation and Soul Care 6,* no. 1 (2013): 93-108.

11. Jürgen Moltmann, "Perichoresis: An Old Magic Word for a New Trinitarian Theology," in *Trinity, Community, and Power,* ed. M. D. Meeks (Nashville, TN: Kingswood, 2006), 111-15.

12. Ibid., 113-15.

13. Joy McDougall, "The Return of Trinitarian Praxis? Moltmann on the Trinity and the Christian Life," *Journal of Religion* 83 (2003): 179.

14. Ibid., 188.

15. Ibid., 188-90.

16. Veli-Matti Karkkainen, *The Trinity: Global Perspectives* (Louisville, KY: Westminster John Knox Press, 2007), 387.

17. Amos Yong, *Renewing Christian Theology* (Waco, TX: Baylor, 2014), 303-04.

18. Jürgen Moltmann, "Perichoresis: An Old Magic Word for a New Trinitarian Theology," in *Trinity, Community, and Power: Mapping Trajectories in Wesleyan Theology,* ed. M. Douglas Meeks (Nashville, TN: Kingswood Books, 2000), 114.

19. Dwight Zschiele, "The Trinity, Leadership, and Power" in *Journal of Religious Leadership,* 6 no. 2 (Fall 2007): 53.

20. Kris Miller, "A Theology of Reconciliation," (Lecture), Lipscomb University, Nashville, TN, February 8, 2016.

21. Ibid.

22. Walter E. Fluker, *They Looked for a City: A Comparative Analysis of the Ideal of Community in the Thought of Howard Thurman and Martin Luther King, Jr.* (New York: University Press of America, 1989), 148.

23. Martin Luther King Jr., *A Testament of Hope*, 20.

24. Peter J. Parris, *Social Teachings of the Black Churches* (Philadelphia, PA: Fortress Press, 1985), 10.

25. J. Richard Middleton, *The Liberating Image: The Imago Dei in Genesis 1* (Grand Rapids, MI: Brazos Press, 2005), 15.

26. Jürgen Moltmann, *The Trinity and the Kingdom: The Doctrine of God* (Minneapolis, MN: Augsburg Fortress, 2005), 105.

27. Martin Luther King Jr., "The Ethical Demands for Integration," in *A Testament of Hope: The Essential Writings of Martin Luther King, Jr.*, ed. James Melvin Washington (San Francisco, CA: Harper & Row, 1986), 119.

28. Ibid.

29. Vanderbilt University Divinity School. "Toward the Elimination of Racism in Vanderbilt Divinity School and the Graduate Department of Religion," divinity.vanderbilt.edu. http://divinity.vanderbilt.edu/student-life/BlackSeminarians-ELIMINATIONOFRACISM-2006.pdf (accessed January 15, 2017).

30. Ibid.

31. J. Todd Billings, *The Word of God for the People of God: An Entry Way to the Theological Interruption of Scripture* (Grand Rapids, MI: Eerdmans, 2010), 89.

32. Donald B. Kraybrill, *The Upside-Down Kingdom* (Harrisburg, VA: Herald Press, 2011), 28.

33. N. T. Wright, *After You Believe: Why Christian Character Matters* (New York: Harper One, 2010), 133.

34. Clarence J. Martin, "The Christian Scriptures and Black Theology," in *What Does It Mean to Be Black and Christian: Pulpit, Pew, and Academy in Dialogue*, ed. Forrest E. Harris Sr. (Nashville, TN: Townsend Press, 1995), 49.

35. James H. Cone, *The Cross and the Lynching Tree* (Maryknoll, NY: Orbis, 2013), 156.

36. Ibid., 165-66.

37. Christopher J. H. Wright, *The Mission of God's People: A Biblical Theology of the Church's Mission* (Grand Rapids, MI: Zondervan, 2010), 89.

38. Jürgen Moltmann, *The Coming of God: Christian Eschatology* (Minneapolis, MN: Fortress Press, 1996), 22.

39. Ibid., 23-24.

40. Ibid., 22.

41. Donald B. Kraybill, *The Upside-Down Kingdom*, rev. ed. (Harrisburg, VA: Herald Press, 2011), 18-19.

42. Ibid., 9.

43. Ibid., 51-82.

44. Luke 22:26.

45. John 17:21.

46. Forrest E. Harris Sr., *Ministry for Social Crisis: Theology and Praxis in the Black Church Tradition* (Macon, GA: Mercer University Press, 1993), 39.

47. Ibid., 30, 37.

48. Ibid., 39.

49. Fong, "Addressing the Issue of Racial Reconciliation," 565.

50. John Stott, *Our Guilty Silence* (Grand Rapids, MI: Eerdmans, 1987), 75.

51. Lesslie Newbigin, *The Gospel in a Pluralist Society* (Grand Rapids, MI: Eerdmans, 1989), 227.

52. Wright, *The Mission of God's People*, 103-04.

53. Goheen, *A Light to the Nations*, 19.

54. Alan J. Roxburgh and Fred Romanuk, *The Missional Leader: Equipping your Church to Reach a Changing World* (Grand Rapids, MI: Brazos Press, 2012), xv.

55. James H. Cone, *Risks of Faith: The Emergence of a Black Theology of Liberation, 1968–1998* (Boston, MA: Beacon Press, 1999), 39.

56. The event was on November 4, 2015, in Jackson, Mississippi. Dr. Young was quoted in "Race, History and Baptist Reconciliation," written by Laurie Goodstein, *New York Times,* January 23, 2016. https://www.nytimes.com/2016/01/24/opinion/sunday/race-history-and-baptist-reconciliation.html?_r=0 (accessed January 14, 2017).

Bibliography

Androzzo, Alma Brizell. "If I Can Help Somebody." *Musicnotes.com*. Bousey & Co. Ltd., 1946.

Bartholomew, Craig G. and Michael W. Goheen. *The True Story of the Whole World: Finding Your Place in the Biblical Drama*. Grand Rapids, MI: Faith Alive Christian Resources, 2009.

Billings, J. Todd. *The Word of God for the People of God: An Entry Way to the Theological Interruption of Scripture*. Grand Rapids, MI: Eerdmans, 2010.

Brueggemann, Walter. "Voices of the Night—Against Justice." In *To Act Justly, Love Tenderly, Walk Humbly*, by Walter Brueggemann, Sharon Park, and Thomas H. Groom. New York: Paulist Press, 1986.

Cone, James. *A Black Theology of Liberation*. Maryknoll, NY: Orbis Books, 1970.

_____. *God of the Oppressed*. Revised Edition. Maryknoll, NY: Orbis Books, 1997.

_____. *Risks of Faith: The Emergence of a Black Theology of Liberation, 1968–1998*. Boston: Beacon Press, 1999.

_____. *The Cross and the Lynching Tree*. Maryknoll, NY: Orbis Books, 2011.

Du Bois, W. E. B. *The Souls of Black Folk*. Chicago, IL: A. C. McClurg & Co., 1903.

Fluker, Walter E. *They Looked for a City: A Comparative Analysis of the Ideal of Community in the Thought of Howard Thurman and*

Martin Luther King, Jr. New York: University Press of America, 1989.

Fong, Bruce W. "Addressing the Issue of Racial Reconciliation according to the Principles of Ephesians 2:11-22." *JETS* 38, no. 4 (1995).

Goheen, Michael W. *A Light to the Nations: The Missional Church and the Biblical Story.* Grand Rapids, MI: Baker Academic, 2011.

Gorman, Michael. *Elements of Biblical Exegesis: A Basic Guide for Students and Ministers.* Revised and Expanded Edition. Grand Rapids, MI: Baker, 2009.

Greene, Kenneth R. "Justice and Racism: What White Churches and Institutions Need to Hear." In *Unfinished Reconciliation: Justice, Racism, and Churches of Christ*, edited by Gary Holloway and John York. Abilene, TX: Abilene Christian University Press, 2013.

Gushee, David P. "Racism and Justice." In *Moral Leadership: News and Notes from the Center for Christian Leadership.* 2001. http://www.uu.edu/centers/christld/moralld/article.cfm?ArticleID=34. Accessed March 1, 2017.

Harris, Forrest E. Sr. *Ministry for Social Crisis: Theology and Praxis in the Black Church Tradition.* Macon, GA: Mercer University Press, 1993.

Harris, Maria. *Proclaim Jubilee! A Spirituality for the Twenty-first Century.* Louisville, KY: Westminster John Knox Press, 1996.

Hjalmarson, Leonard E. "A Trinitarian Spirituality of Mission," *Journal of Spiritual Formation and Soul Care* 6, no. 1 (2013).

Karkkainen, Veli-Matti. *The Trinity: Global Perspectives.* Louisville, KY: Westminster John Knox Press, 2007.

King, Martin Luther Jr. *Where Do We Go from Here: Chaos or Community?* Boston: Beacon Press, 1968.

_____. *Strength to Love.* New York: Harper & Row, 1963.

_____. *A Testament of Hope: The Essential Writings and Speeches of Martin Luther King, Jr.,* edited by James W. Washington. San Francisco, CA: Harper & Row, 1986.

_____. *Stride toward Freedom: The Montgomery Story.* New York: Harper Collins Press, Reprint, 1987.

_____. *Address at the Religious Leaders Conference* May 11, 1959. https://kinginstitute.stanford.edu/king-papers/documents/address-religious-leaders-conference-11-may-1959. Accessed February 28, 2017.

_____. "Black Power Defined." In *I Have a Dream: Writings and Speeches That Changed the World,* edited by James M. Washington. New York: Harper, 1992.

_____. "The Ethical Demands for Integration." In *A Testament of Hope: The Essential Writings of Martin Luther King, Jr.,* edited by James Melvin Washington. San Francisco, CA: Harper & Row, 1986.

_____. "Facing the Challenge of a New Age." In *Phylon* (1957).

_____. "MIA Mass Meeting at Holt Street Baptist Church." In *The Papers of Martin Luther King, Jr.,* edited by Clayborne Carson. Berkeley, CA: University of California Press, 1992.

Kraybrill, Donald B. *The Upside-Down Kingdom.* Harrisonburg, VA: Herald Press, 2011.

Martin, Clarence J. "The Christian Scriptures and Black Theology." In *What Does It Mean to Be Black and Christian: Pulpit, Pew, and*

Academy in Dialogue, edited by Forrest E. Harris, Sr. Nashville, TN: Townsend Press, 1995.

Mays, Benjamin E. *The Negro's God As Reflected In His Literature*. New York: Atheneum, 1969.

McDougall, Joy. "The Return of Trinitarian Praxis? Moltmann on the Trinity and the Christian Life." *Journal of Religion* 83 (2003).

Middleton, J. Richard. *The Liberating Image: The* Imago Dei *in Genesis 1*. Grand Rapids, MI: Brazos Press, 2005.

Miller, Kris. "A Theology of Reconciliation" (Lecture). At Lipscomb University, Nashville, TN, February 8, 2016.

Moltmann, Jürgen. "Perichoresis: An Old Magic Word for a New Trinitarian Theology." In *Trinity, Community, and Power*, edited by M. D. Meeks. Nashville, TN: Kingswood, 2006.

———. *The Trinity and the Kingdom: The Doctrine of God*. Minneapolis, MN: Fortress Press, 2005.

———. *The Coming of God: Christian Eschatology*. Minneapolis, MN: Fortress Press, 1996.

National Education Association. *Education and Racism*. Washington, DC: National Education Association, 1973.

Newbigin, Lesslie. *The Gospel in a Pluralist Society*. Grand Rapids, MI: Eerdmans, 1989.

Parris, Peter J. *Social Teachings of the Black Churches*. Philadelphia, PA: Fortress Press, 1985.

Rivers, Eugene. "The Responsibility of Evangelical Intellectuals in the Age of White Supremacy." In *The Gospel in Black & White: Theological Resources for Racial Reconciliation*, edited by Dennis L. Okholm. Downers Grove, IL: InterVarsity Press, 1997.

Roberts, J. Deotis. *A Black Political Theology.* Philadelphia, PA: Westminster Press, 1974.

Roxburgh, Alan J. *Missional: Joining God in the Neighborhood.* Grand Rapids, MI: Eerdmans, 1998.

Roxburgh, Alan J. and Fred Romanuk. *The Missional Leader: Equipping Your Church to Reach a Changing World.* Grand Rapids, MI: Brazos Press, 2012.

Stott, John. *The Contemporary Christian: An Urgent Plea for Double Listening.* Leicester, UK: InterVarsity Press, 1992.

_____. *Our Guilty Silence.* Grand Rapids, MI: Eerdmans, 1987.

Vanderbilt University Divinity School. "Toward the Elimination of Racism in Vanderbilt School and the Graduate Department of Religion." divinity.vanderbilt.edu. http://divinity.vanderbilt.edu/student-life/BlackSeminarians-ELIMINATIONOFRACISM-2006.pdf (accessed January 15, 2017).

Washington, Booker T. *Up from Slavery.* New York: Oxford University Press, 1901.

Wolterstorff, Nicholas. *Justice: Rights and Wrongs.* Princeton, NJ: Princeton University Press, 2008.

Wright, Christopher J. H. *The Mission of God: Unlocking the Bible's Grand Narrative.* Downers Grove, IL: IVP Academic, 2006.

_____. *The Mission of God's People: A Biblical Theology of the Church's Mission.* Grand Rapids, MI: Zondervan, 2010.

Wright, N. T. *The New Testament and the People of God*, London: SPCK Publishing, 1992.

_____. *After You Believe: Why Christian Character Matters.* New York: Harper One, 2010.

Yancey George. *Beyond Racial Gridlock: Embracing Mutual Responsibility*. Westmont, IL: IVP Books, 2006.

Yong, Amos. *Renewing Christian Theology*. Waco, TX: Baylor, 2014.

Young, Jerry. Quoted in "Race, History and Baptist Reconciliation." *New York Times*, January 23, 2016. https://www.nytimes.com/2016/01/24/opinion/sunday/race-history-and-baptist-reconciliation.html?_r=0. Accessed January 14, 2017

Zschiele, Dwight. "The Trinity, Leadership, and Power." *Journal of Religious Leadership*, 6 no. 2 (Fall 2007).